Lingo Dingo and the Turkish astronaut

Written by Mark Pallis
Illustrated by James Cottell

For my awesome sons Oscar and Felix - MP

For Sophia - JC

LINGO DINGO AND THE TURKISH ASTRONAUT

Story edited by Natascha Biebow, Blue Elephant Storyshaping
With special thanks to Esra Sagol Rehill for the Turkish translation
First Printing, 2022
ISBN: 978-1-915337-01-6
markpallis.com

Lingo Dingo and the Turkish astronaut

Written by Mark Pallis
Illustrated by James Cottell

NEU WESTEND
— PRESS —

This is Lingo. She's a Dingo and she loves helping.

Anyone. Anytime. Anyhow.

It was a big day.

Lingo's friend, Sue, was off on a mission to the International Space Station. Departure was in one minute and Sue was running late.

"Look out for the banana skin!" cried Lingo.

"I'll be OK, but the mission is over," said Sue.

"I can help!" said Lingo.

But there were only thirty
seconds to launch:
hurry Lingo!

Quick as a shooting star, Lingo climbed up into the rocket.

"Don't forget this. It's a battery for the Space Station," said Sue.

The countdown began: Five, four...

Lingo buckled up.
3...
She felt nervous.
2...
1...
Blast off!

"Merhaba!" said an astronaut. "Benim adım Rex. Ben bir astronotum."
Lingo tried a reply in Turkish, "Benim adım Lingo."

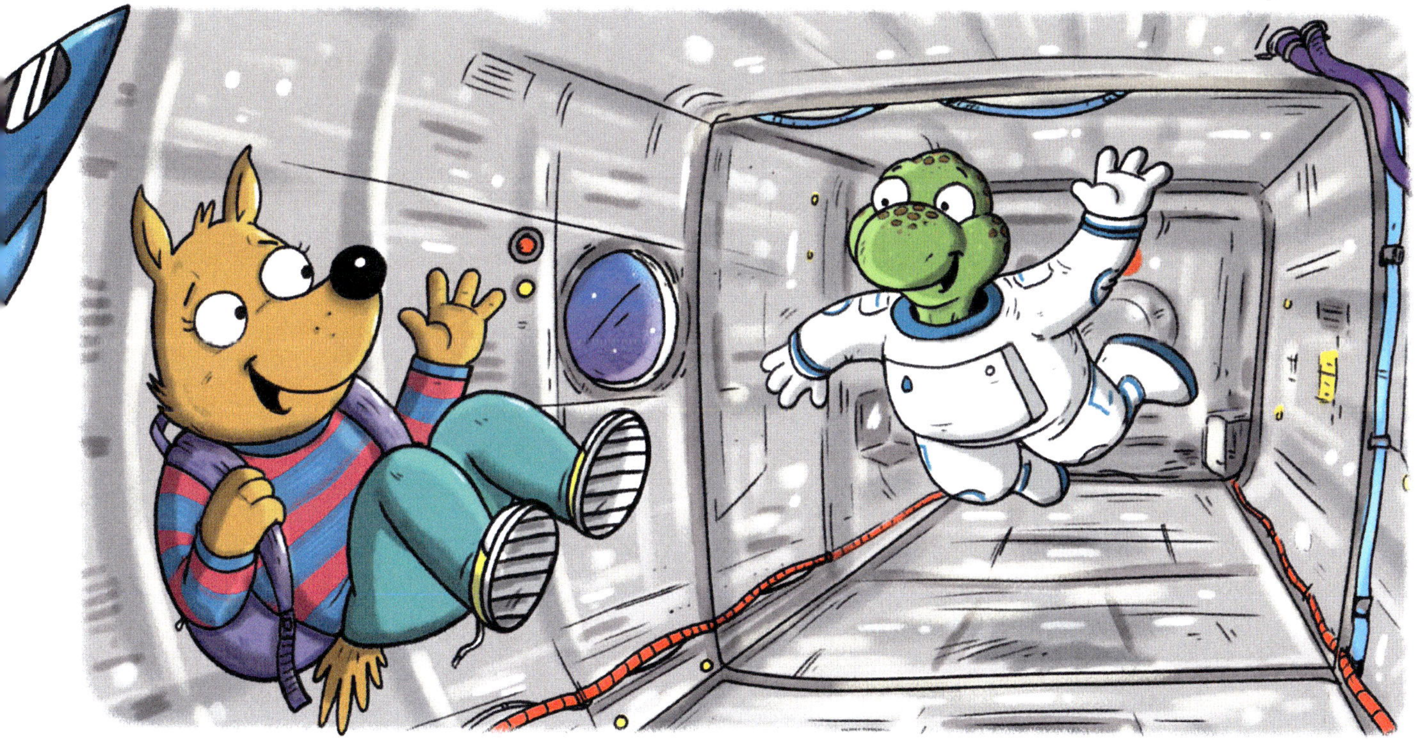

Merhaba = Welcome; **Benim adım** = My name is; **Ben bir astronotum** = I am an astronaut

gel = come; **tuvalet** = the toilet; **laboratuvar** = the laboratory
Yatak odası = the bedroom; **Ve benim oyuncak ayım** = and my teddybear

Suddenly a BEEPING blared out!
"Yeni pili getirdin mi?" asked Rex.
Lingo wasn't sure what 'pil' meant. She checked her pockets.

yeni pili getirdin mi? = have you got the new battery?
pil = battery

A fishing rod?

Olta mı? Hayır.

A camera?

Fotoğraf makinesi mi? Hayır.

This?

Evet, pil!

"Uzay kıyafetlerini giy."

It was time to open the airlock.

olta mı = a fishing rod; **hayır** = no
fotoğraf makinesi mi = a camera; **evet** = yes; **uzay kıyafetlerini giy!** = space suit on!

"Sola çevir," said Rex, pointing to the handle.

Lingo turned it right. "Sağa değil, sola!" cried Rex. Lingo turned it left and the hatch swung open.

sola çevir = turn it left; **sağa** = right; **sola** = left

Space was waiting for them!
They got straight to work changing the battery.
“Tornavidayı verir misin lütfen?” said Rex.

Lingo passed Rex the screwdriver and he screwed the new battery into place.

Tornavidayı = screwdriver; **Tornavidayı verir misin lütfen** = will you pass me the screwdriver please

"Başardık! Çak bir beşlik," he said.

Lingo realised Rex wanted a high five.

Success!

Lingo called Sue with the good news:

Başardık! = We did it!; **Çak bir beşlik** = Give me five

The view was incredible.

Rex pointed out all the things to see.

"Güneş."

"Dünya."

Dünya = the earth; **Güneş** = the sun

Yıldızlar = the stars; **Ay** = the moon; **Robotik kol** = the robotic arm

“Oyuncak ayım!” cried Rex.
Rex’s teddy must have floated out of the airlock.
“Robotik kolu kullan,” he said.

Lingo was going to use the robotic arm.

Oyuncak ayım = my teddy; **Robotik kolu kullan** = use the robotic arm

Rex called out the directions: “Yukarı. Aşağı.
Çok yaklaştın. Yakala!”

Lingo closed the hand...

but Teddy was too far away!

“Hayır! Oyuncak ayı kayboldu,”
cried Rex.

“I can help,” said Lingo.

She noticed something
else floating nearby.

Yukarı = up; **Aşağı** = down; **Çok yaklaştın** = almost; **Yakala** = grab;
Oyuncak ayı kayboldu = My teddybear is lost

Her fishing rod!

She swung the hook
out into space.

Şans dile = fingers crossed

Arkadaşım = my friend; **Hadi kutlayalım** = let's party

Rex pressed a button and funky music boomed out.

Time to bust some zero gravity dance moves.

“Ben dans ediyorum, sen dans ediyorsun, oyuncak ayı dans ediyor, biz dans ediyoruz.” laughed Rex.

Ben dans ediyorum = I am dancing; **sen dans ediyorsu** = you are dancing
oyuncak ayı dans ediyor = my teddy is dancing; **biz dans ediyoruz** = we are dancing

"Gülümse!" said Rex,
and took a photo.

Gülümse = smile

"Susadın mı?" asked Rex. He squeezed big blobs of water over to Lingo. "Bu su," he said. "Acıktın mı?" asked Rex.

Susadın mı? = are you thirsty?; **Bu su** = it is water; **Acıktın mı?** = are you hungry?

Ben de = me too; **Dondurma** = ice cream

Uzayı seviyorum = I love space

İyi uykular = goodnight

Learning to love languages

An additional language opens a child's mind, broadens their horizons and enriches their emotional life. Research has shown that the time between a child's birth and their sixth or seventh birthday is a "golden period" when they are most receptive to new languages. This is because they have an in-built ability to distinguish the sounds they hear and make sense of them. The Story-powered Language Learning Method taps into these natural abilities.

How the story-powered language learning method works

We create an emotionally engaging and funny story for children and adults to enjoy together, just like any other picture book. Studies show that social interaction, like enjoying a book together, is critical in language learning.

Through the story, we introduce a relatable character who speaks only in the new language. This helps build empathy and a positive attitude towards people who speak different languages. These are both important aspects in laying the foundations for lasting language acquisition in a child's life.

As the story progresses, the child naturally works with the characters to discover the meanings of a wide range of fun new words. Strategic use of humour ensures that this subconscious learning is rewarded with laughter; the child feels good and the first seeds of a lifelong love of languages are sown.

For more information and free learning resources visit www.neuwestendpress.com

You can learn more words and phrases with these hilarious, heartwarming stories from NEU WESTEND — PRESS —

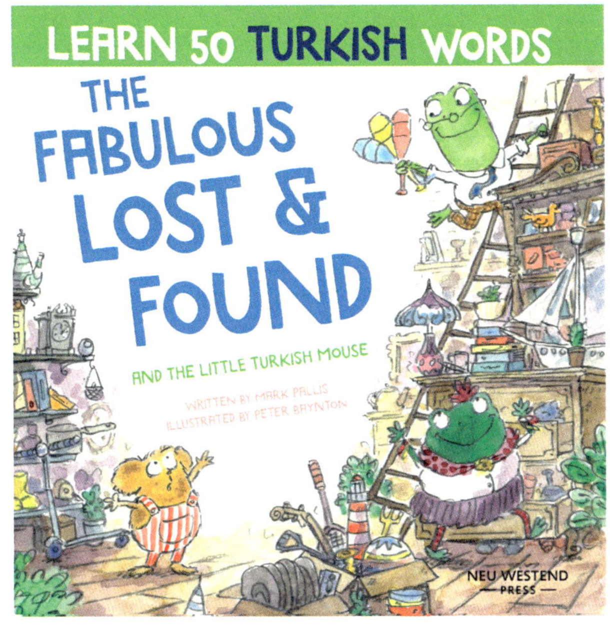

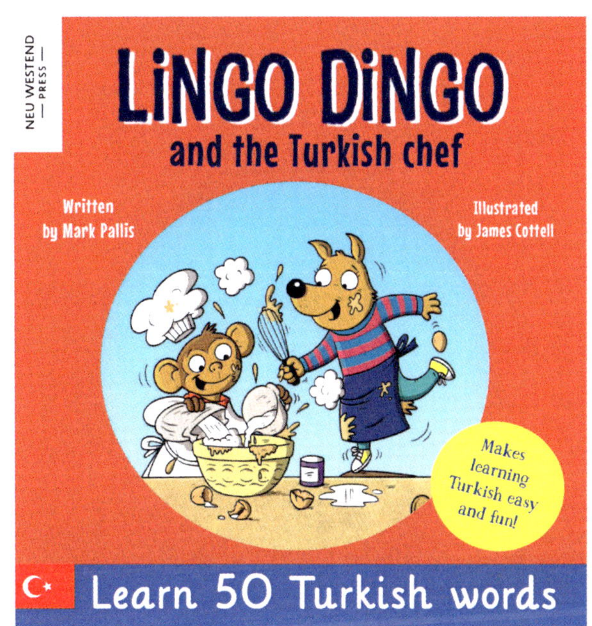

@MARK_PALLIS on twitter
www.markpallis.com

To download your FREE certifcate, and more cool stuff, visit www.neuwestendpress.com

@jamescottell on INSTAGRAM
www.jamescottellstudios.com

“I want people to be so busy laughing, they don’t realise they’re learning!”

Mark Pallis

Crab and Whale is the bestselling story of how a little Crab helps a big Whale. It’s carefully designed to help even the most energetic children find a moment of calm and focus. It also includes a special mindful breathing exercise and affirmation for children.
(Also available in Turkish as Yengeç ile Balina)
Featured as one of Mindful.org’s
‘Seven Mindful Children’s books’

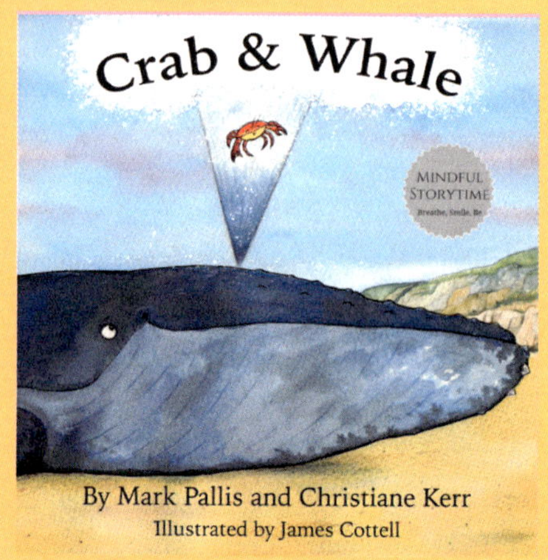

Do you call them hugs or cuddles?

In this funny, heartwarming story, you will laugh out loud as two loveable gibbons try to figure out if a hug is better than a cuddle and, in the process, learn how to get along.

A perfect story for anyone who loves a hug (or a cuddle!)

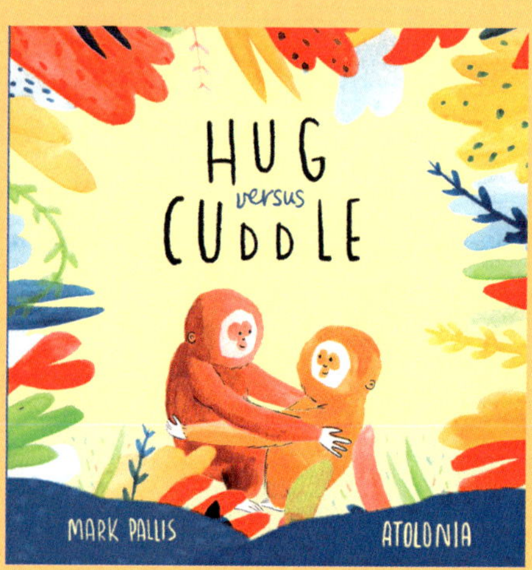

www.markpallis.com

Made in the USA
Monee, IL
08 January 2024

51374008R00021